SINEW AND SEA

JayLynn Fraye-Rummel

ISBN: 979-8-218-27702-4

Cover Art by Kamryn Rose Boykin
Cover Graphic Design by Trinity Phan-Low

Printed and Distributed by IngramSparks

— • —

— • —

DEDICATION

To my 17-year-old self, who never thought she would get this far.
A special thanks to those who believed in me, despite my many set-
backs: Kamryn Boykin, Trinity Phan-Low, Rogelio Lopez, and my
mother. Thank you for never giving up on me.
And even though we don't talk anymore, Alyssa Stabley.

— • —

THIS BOOK CONTAINS SENSITIVE MATERIAL RELATING TO:

RELIGIOUS CRITICISM
TRAUMA AND PTSD
ABUSE
SEX
MOURNING
VIOLENCE
DISABILITY AND BODY HORROR
PLEASE TAKE CARE WHILE READING.

—•—

—•—

CONTENTS

FATE

And even so, the gold in my veins cries
    for desperate relief.
    An Achillean Burn,
    The heroic grin,
    For something more than creating
    —but to inspire that which seems impossible.
    To turn tragedies into victories.

    Must sacrifice be met with one's remiss?
    For the fate of Fallen's champion ends with sorrow,
    To give such joy, must the hero be eclipsed
    Balanced by the scales, to match the bliss?
    A punishment, perhaps, for testing fate
    —a sorrow that burns even the great.

—◦—

WE DON'T GO FOR THE GOOD ONES.

Our mothers' hollow breaths echo with empty promises,
   Laughs they lost, sentences on settling.
   Emotions aren't always their strong suit.

   Pushing on the playground spills a story of love;
   Of young hearts like scraped knees,
   Too torn by turbulence to realize that the hand that holds is the one
that harms.
   So what of heart-torn hands that push and shove,
   only to receive such pain in return?
   If they start the fight, you finish it.
   Do they understand that we were taught to hit back?
   To scream fire instead of help,
   Yet love the hand that feeds, despite the food being cold.

   So why do we always choose the bad ones?
   Affection laced in every shove, stinging fingers and poisoned hearts.
   But *we* were taught of violence prolonged.
   That there is evil in our hands, but boys just matured wrong.
   As if Nice isn't standard.
   As if Nice means Kind,
   As if Nice is purely Physical,

Ignoring manipulation and mental grime,
Pretending that guilt is a tool, made to climb
the ladder of our ribs into molded breasts.
Because what are the teachings of love, if not
playground pushes
and being possessed?

— ◦ —

GUILT

Guilt was something never so pretty,
    For ever seed grows anxiety
    And sparks a fire that dries the sea,
    Flesh peeling under desperate wants,
    And feeling as if it's not enough.

    What is it, but something to another?
    A force much stronger than desperate lovers,
    It only benefits the one
    To cry to kingdom come.
    So what of the danger that crawls within,
    The darker days of victimized vice"
    Banish the betrayer from these halls,
    You think you can feel,
    But the wall never falls.

— ● —

GOLDEN FINGERS

I am not a hero.
  No golden fingers,
  No strength past what I've spent.
  I could have been one, I think,
  Before what they've done.
  Not anymore.

  No heroes,
  No villains, even,
  I've burnt out my spite.

  Just brine confined,
  in sinew and skin,
  Too scared and worn for light.

—·—

IN THE NAME OF

Religions were never so pretty.
    Every myth and god,
    Every book of silver light
    glimmers only of the blood-written words that never go dry.
    Every drop of ichor-licked ink shines
    Like a star

                          The Morning?—

    Or a lightning-struck fire
    or the gleam of his cross necklace as he leans over your sweet,
untouched body
    Says his palm shall only touch the pure and holy.

You don't speak up.
    It's bad if you're not pure and holy.
              And the ink drips from his fingers as he
                     writes the word of—
We laugh at myths while regarding our falsities as fact,
    Ares is our god of war—
    Of cruel smiles and golden tongue rings.
               And the Ink drips from every sword
                  and bullet-born battle
                   fought in the name of—

Hades, not the gem-crusted god of dead, but the
enemy of Yahweh

And the Ink drips
from the whips wrought
against children in the name of—

Isis, no Egyptian goddess, but the name of
once-funded enemies.

The blood and violence and
war and dead
The threatening of those
with knees unbent.

If the gods are real, they played us well—
Raising rodent-run slaughterhouses,
Who don execution unto themselves.
Every piece and opinion,
Thin-paged book and bind,
The stories always glimmer
Because the blood never dries.

In the Name of God,
Amen.

SECURING SAFETY

Through it all,
    I remember my violence.
    The desire to have my heart torn free,
    placed out of its misery,
    Grasped tight with choking breaths,
    and ground into simplicity.
    Tintcured overrides finding stability.
    As if quaking claws can't break concrete,
    or a Last Restort's finality.

MOTHER

My mother is buried in my skin.
   Mannerisms, irritations, fierce independence,
   and generational trauma pour through my marrow and press on my
throat;
   To stand so strong in the face of fraternal violence,
   Science and suspicion gripping entrails,
   Choking down food and casting eyes at those who wish not to help
themselves.

   To be angry, and cold, and standing off against the mirror as my eyes
match a scale,
   hating that which extended judgment fails,
   and weighing false figments of cerebral failure.
   I am our prickled green wire, barbed poison bind,
   Our disordered tastes,
   And sadness running over silver screens we hide between.

—·—

TRAGEDIES (1)

Are we tragedies?
    All of us upon this land
    who bend their backs and force their hands,
    Creatures of arrogance, greed, and pride,
    great creators, beautiful minds

    When the final curtain falls,
    The watchers file into appalled silence,
    Of ancient cities of oil and steel,
    Fruit swept away in circuit fields,
    The nectar of our names,
    plucked pixel by pixel by away.

VENOM

And that was all the rift required.
    A little tear—
    A pull in the fabric—
    To know it was there.

    If I am not what I've endured,
    I carry every angry note,
    The weight of sin,
    lain as a cloak of cruelty to keep me warm,
    to melt into my bones and become the sinew of my soul.

    The poison fed to me
    Made me not immune—
    But spread roots in my spirit,
    Becoming venom.

WRITING DOESN'T PAY THE RENT

I was writing stories.
   Pretty things, melodies,
   Carving my destinies,
   Months ago the exhaust wasn't quite the same.
   I didn't miss voices called my name,
   And maybe I was in a better place—
   I could pay rent, had my own space—
   Do you know what it's like to not create?
   A primal calling so deep in your bones,
   The thing I finally embraces and loved, turning to
   ash as I sent sparks above,
   And burn.

   For a better future? Or a washed-up fantasy of inconsistency.
   Gig work and hearsay, wrapped in shitty days,
   How can one create with bills to pay?
   When I knock cohesion from my hands like bullets from wet, oiled
pans,
   As there was never any room to fly because suffering is a box, but to
sit is to survive.

   Wings scrape hallowed walls,

Gasping for breath in a dried-out sea,
Where devoid projects must be laid to rest.
Nine months too long,
to have only divestment.

—·—

CAUSTIC COMFORTS

There is too much—
   Too little—
   Too late—
   For words to flow or bed escape,

   A chemical pressure along the head,
   Resurfaced memories left for dead,
   Exhaustion's bite takes your hand
   and leads you to familiar lands.

   But bottled green is half the joy,
   When seas turn black
   and comfort is a play—
   Home is a place you build in your chest,
   With bridges connecting treehouse nests,
   as roots spread,
   bringing you another's air.

   But fire burns like gasoline rivers,
   And family is fickle when comfort quivers.

— · —

ODYSSEY

There's a certain fear in safety,
   A certain softness in the sad,
   While breath catches in the chest and
   a cage of unknowns and rewritten stories
   will bleed like a maiden's ever-iron breast,
   And the Ink Stains on my hands will smother yours
   like self-fulfilling prophecies—
   those of mazes and odysseys—
   Where no being will ever learn to let themselves be happy.
   Absorbing the weight of another's hell,
   but shouldering the weight well.

GARDENS AND GRAVES

There is a time to be soft,
    For silken slips and green tean,
    face masks and subtlety.

    But this is not that time.
    Tear lace away and bear your fists like claws,
    The power that lies in being hurt—
    in being over being hurt—
    Tear the crown from golden pedestals,
    as victories should be screamed like they're sensual—

    You're allowed to be hellfire and hydrangeas,
    You're allowed starlight and snowdrops.

— · —

REJECTION, IMPLIED

What is the definition of a rejection as such,
   The lack of desire, or touch,
   What difference from that of platonic whims that
   hold hearts close, but never closer—
   How does one avoid pressing when such matters are hardpressed?

   In echoing hearts: crevices pushing out air,
   Love without show, breaking in Philia's tow,
   The tug of the throat pulled into strings,
   Every chord and flicker of flesh broken between bone,
   Should such Mourning be so quickly assigned? Placed as desired for
the throes of Powers
   that may be?
   Or perhaps, it is beckoned for free.
   Wretchedly clung to delusions—What is romance if not a friend?
   All the dame heartache without a finger laid,
   If desperation is what cloys so strong, how is sorrow to be fixed?
   A desire to be free of it relieves no pain.

— · —

How sad, in the eternity of things:

that prime is only held so close to youth—
    For years of life to be so heavily subdued
    As if sturdiness is a curse sent unto those who have found peace,
    As if complacency is the same thing as being free.

    Dreams need not dissolve under the weight of age,
    Nor should beauty break with grey,
    For what can match consistency?
    What bliss can be attained in a lack of stability?
    Why spit in the face of those who dare to breathe,
    Who find comfort in foundation,
    Who dares to find happiness after they teethe the infancy of ages
before 30.

    Youth,
    Sold as your only success and sin,
    though passion only expires when it's stolen
    by office chairs and elder glares—
    sitting ducks who envy the sky high ring,
    claiming melted-wax dream,
    Unable to reach beyond what was taught.

Your life will not end after a quarter.
One's existence is more than childhood splendor.

--.--

FROM MOUNTAIN TO MOLEHILL

I apologize to every girl
    Whose words I turned away
    In favor of the cold of his earring on my tongue,
    And the scars his fingers dug into my ventricles.

    Heal as they may,
    the lessons eternally remain.

    I'm climbing the mountain of your words
    that you so graciously quaked to create—
    And once I reach that summit
    Your name will not scare me anymore.

—·—

PAST LIFE

I wonder if this life will fall to defeat,
 Will my soul move from such sadness and sorrow?
 Catching on wings that burn under brightened skies
 And delivering my beating break to the shores I once lapped,
 as waves of salt and sand—

 Shall another cycle fall upon me if I am not healed of frustration and
somber?
 As rage courses through my teeth,
 Gums bloody with earnest deceit
 that this life will be my last.

 And what then, of my harrowed psyche,
 will remain on the crumbles of this place,
 As soil falls to human flame:
 The burning of the sacred vale
 between stars and the seraphic.

— • —

DIVINITY

It's a blessing, they say, to be made of ember and flame.
    A comfort to rock with the soul of the sea,
    to heal the hurt and only succeed,
    To be the mother goddess in a child's body,
    Sacrificing skin to warm the masses,
    Burning brighter with fiery passion until your body is a pyre, and
the world a maze.
    It's a crime to be exhausted at such a young age.
    I was not built to carry the world.
    The bursas bulge with misplaced ministrations,
    Nails peeling back from blisters and pain,
    Throats flake with cinders as the esophagus smokes,
    Wave polluted with rotted expectations.

    Carve every sin from my skin,
    and when all that is left is exasperation and contempt,
    do not mind the calcified conflagration of others' rapacity.
    With my charcoal crust of ember and rust, and
    smoldering steam.

— • —

WHEREIN PASSION LIES THE PAIN

In the wake of everything we've ever known,
    Should ichor stain my teeth in the memory of you,
    May the stones of Scylla hold my fallen form.
    That which is worm from wars of self and sorrow,
    Of gifted rancor nesting between the needs to be yet soft,
    and sturdy.
    Of being protection and pacifism.

    Should I lay, dressed in wax, beside the tossing sea,
    Bones for the birds,
    Will I remember wanting peace?
    Impossible feats, when those who wage wish you deceased.

NATURE AND NEUTRALITY

Is it a sin to crave that which goes unseen?
    For those beliefs that echo in our limbs as we beg for release.
    For a Genesis that explains how such pain shall repeat—
    This fury begs the desperation of opposite extremes,
    Devotion in trust, or the rejection of such omnipotent things.
    What is a deity but one's own belief?
    And to throng the throes of such theories into the throats of those
who have broken free is an onslaught of terror in the name of peace.

    And where shall I sit in the guilt of craving something more,
    With no trust in beings that live only in credence,
    as if faith is enough to turn me to tyrants who threaten love with
violence,
    At least those of antiquity do not deny they are sanies and grief.

    Beg me a nihilist, but I refuse to abide in complacent silence,
    So where do I find the comfort of more
    beyond the physical terrene doors,
    That hold the soul in the confines of the Earth?

    At least elements are true,
    in nature and neutrality.

A flame is not at fault for burning eternally.

DRYAD AND THE NYMPH

Dip your fingers in my lip,
   And pull the sorrow from my breaking neck,
   That which folds to desires of a spirit untold—
   A ghost of the past.

   A time and place, you've said,
   For creatures to haunt us whole.
   Drag the shipwreck of my psyche into sun,
   And wipe the brine from my brow.
   A corrosive thing, meant to carry casualties,
   Was sinking a choice unseen?
   Maybe just an aspect of existing.
   But even so, you take my tongue
   and place nectar to my teeth.

   The coast will meet the forest,
   for the dryad and the nymph to feast.

—·—

GODS CANNOT IMAGINE,

the Unforgiving Grief.
    The stutter of every thumb-placed thread of words,
    The desire-drenched thief of desolation.

    I don't know if we could still be friends.
    It doesn't change the need to know you again.

— • —

I Can't Help

but to remember you,
    The echo of you in my crystal cage home,
    A storm I could never touch.
    Lightning licking the sky, but never my skin,
    Bellicose winds,
    And there was little I could do
    to escape you.

    And here we are.
    Metal memories and oxidating wanderlust,
    How could I forget you,
    When you gave me so many things to love?

    Well.

    Not every end is satisfying.

What is God to the Waves?

To my imperceptible wrath?
  What is that strength to the pressure in my tonsils,
  Curling muscle and shredding skin,
  Checking out of this lifetime like a book past due,
  With shelves too high to climb.

— • —

MATHIAS

There's lightning in his veins,
    I've said it before.
    Skin-struck waves and storms.
    It feels of home,
    Of warmth,
    A gentle reprise when I remember what it feels like to be happy,
    To have hope,
    When smiles burn into my cheeks with melting heat.

    And I cannot lift the sorrow from your soul,
    Nor can I bear the world,
    But I can be the lighthouse that reaches into the dark
    Holding a hand to your heart,
    And, perhaps, I can be warmth after frozen rain.
    A gentle fire—not quite chaos, not quite tame,
    Giving back to the Northern Light,
    guiding me home in the dark of the night.

—·—

I Think I'm Lonely Tonight,

Like the feeling of your favorite show, playing to a crowd that never
watches.
    When your voice is drowned by backseat blearing.
    A/C fans and coveted conversations.
    Ideas stolen, and half-hearted texts that you know aren't cruel,
    But sometimes you wonder
    if they hate you, too.

    And maybe it's the principle of it.
    The miracle of melancholy,

    the fire-starter sadness that comes with isolation,
    drowning alone in summer sweat,
    scorching hesitation like trees—
    to germinate and grow anew.

Lay your head in their sweet shade, and don't try to forget.
You will always know that hold in your chest.

— • —

SUSPECTING LOVE LIKE A HOAX

And how, prey tell, do I write of you?
  Of messy feelings,
  Tangled threads of thoughts to undo—
  Is it love?
  Or a more simple thing,
  A skin-stroked bond of simplicity;

  Where does the line blur into throat-clawed gazes
  Trembling lips upon each other's faces and—
  Where do my liberties meet,
  In what I may say or do.

— • —

LIGHTNING SHOULDN'T STRIKE TWICE,

but hasn't that been proven myth?
   I've gotten too comfortable
   dancing across the line
   Letting exaggeration take my flesh,
   burning the brick, and
   melting the mortar.
   Tearing down defenses for dopamine hits.
   Though, I suppose zeal has always been my vice.

   And electrocution cut the power,
   as turbulence drowns my pleas,
   I know there is peace in these choices,
   but I sit, bleeding, on my knees.

— • —

I THINK I COULD HAVE HAD IT, ONCE.

Another world, with another me,
  Porch-light paradise and tea.

  What is it, to be born with mourning?
  To have heartstrings tug along with tragedy;
  For such themes to be bread into your bone.
  I don't believe in fate, in the broad sense,
  But maybe a few,
  A handful, or two,
  Are meant to bear a blight that bleeds along the moor.

  A docking home for abandoned woes,
  Where sorrow meets the shore.

— • —

I THINK IT SCARES HER.

How deep this thread runs through my fingers,
  How the longing runs along pad-print lines,
  Every grove and grimace individual,
  Unique,
  And when sorrow is embedded into that which portrays you?
  Such worry revolved in acidic pits of stomached wine,
  Like rum and stardust combined,
  When comfort creatures mold into the echoes of your sadness,
  And the fibers flaying from ferocious hearts bind into your soul.
  What is a character, if not a confession?

— • —

WULF

There is a primal understanding,
   between the Lion and the King,
   A staggered catch to feral souls,
   Breaths mistaken for judgment
   Toll the ever night,
   But bless the brute that matches your own—

There is a tremor in our calcified cages,
   Cracks that tear the moment they are healed.
   What relief, to share ichor-welt skin,
   Forged into our levin seal.

I DON'T THINK I EVER LEARNED TO MOURN.

Up, blink, tear
　　out gentle roots, and breakthrough.
　　No blood seen
　　should bring peace,
　　but Childhood is buried in the hatred of my tears,
　　Scorning the sadness with the ever-present tithe of needing to be
better.

　　What could I offer, except for myself?
　　My worth,
　　Skin and song, all bleed out upon
　　a never-solid ground.
　　The resonant ring of peace
　　Never once appearing to me.

How quaint,

To worship the world,
  and nothing beyond.

  What freedom,
  To feel the elements' embrace.
  To touch the leaves' distaste and joy.
  When the dice bend to the story's whim.
  When it is free from good and bad because it simply just *is.*
  It has no price to pay to remain in glory,
  No threats of torture following death,
  With no need for prayers or placatory breath.

— · —

BLOOM

There are fresh hands churning the soil.
    They grow and stretch from rooted ruin
    and Sing upon the slough.

    Do you feel their fing e r t ips?
    The solid snap of supple drumming,
    Slipping and catching in its careful climb
    As it rakes against your dermis?

Do y ou fe el th e m?
    Do

        y ou

                se aring into your ski n?

Or as they bl o om?

— ◦ —

ZEALOUS

Zeal is a shock to the system.
   And I, only ever over,
   Have carried electricity in my veins.

   Though gentle touch lays out of range,
   A white-hot fire burns inside,
   a mix of warmth and comfort and pain

   Is this passion new?
   An intense desire for two, three, a million—
   A closeness buried down and slain—

   By carelessness of my own,
   I retract,
   Fear as a bridle to my brain

   And though it is strange,
   Such affections are not oft made tame,

   A twisted cage of bristle and thorn,
   a Lover's blade and Executioner's bane.

— • —

HOAX, RECOGNIZED

And sometimes I suppose, the spark dies.
   No more lightning, no northern stars,
   Just a lingering, lost feeling as you let love crush from your palm

— · —

I FEEL MY MOTHER'S FLESH

in the bed of my nails
    Pushing keratin from skin and flooding my palms with collective blood,
    The mirror shattered as we pick apart shards of self,
    Every shared slip, falling between us in quarters and halves,
    And I wonder what it feels like to be whole.

    What is convoluted conviction, if not a place to freeze?
    An empty bed for sorrow-soaked heads.

— • —

(FUNCTIO LAESA)

How can I write when my hands are a carcass,
   A cadaver of broken bones,
   With rubor flesh and frozen calor.
   To think,
   25 would be the year of the crone
   Wet with salves that make no home.

WHAT WE LEARN TO HIDE

It wasn't about the car.
   It was not that you are a tree of wealth and valor,
   Not a crime against your character, not a stab into thy psyche.

   It was the hope that hides in the young.
   The fall on fractured concrete,
   Skin scraped and torn anew:

   It was the hand held up,
   Hoping for a nest that was never made,
   Breaking backs for wasted talent and shattered dreams.

   It was the hand held up,
   begging for relief
   slapped down at the sign of panic—
   Abandonment

PEDESTAL

It is like watching a seaside city sink,
   The rise and fall of burdened euphoria.
   To be so grand,
   And so frail.

— • —

AN URCHIN HIDES IN ACUPUNCTURE POINTS

Finding each hollow pore to place its poison,
  And there is nothing you can do.

  Boxed tendrils make home of your joints,
  Filling the space of broken rubber bands—
  A bosun stepping into place of blue-collar breakthroughs—
  Without a single hand to bend the plates of broken bone back into
place.

— • —

Polarizing Parasites

Why do I apologize
    For the knife you plunge in me every time he shows his face?
    Every time you accept him with open arms and grace?
    Despite my skin crawling away?
    And my bones breaking down into hollow hairline cervices?
    And the blood filling my mouth
    From bitten lips
    From the nails scratching against the door I'm trapped behind,
    Because his presence makes my body burn
    With every sense of fear and disgust.

    Why don't you fucking understand?
    I've told you what it does to me,
    How I avoid his face,
    Scrub the image with bleach
    Scratch the eyes out with a knife
    When my chest caves in
    And breaks apart
    Piece by piece
    As the acid of my memories makes me shake.

— • —

THERE IS SOMETHING INSIDE ME.

There is rot here
    In the veins and bones and sacred thoughts
    Blacked Spots
    Where mildew lies in the lymph vessels,
    And mold crawls.

    Its hundreds of legs skitter and hop;
    Slipping needles into sinuses.
    It calls this a hug. It says how it loves to cradle your face, and catch you when you stumble and shreds your skin for ancientvowSAN-DITREACHESANDREACHESANDREACHESANDREACHESANDREACHESAND

— • —

I SIT,

Silent and still,
   Working in midnight smoking nests

   As if hallowed hearts will arise,
   As if wandering eggs will hatch.

   Seeding interest into empty breaths,
   Hands numb and oiled
   like post-work pores.

— • —

It Grows Beyond Elder Gardens

To think
   my ministrations
   could be contained by ancient wine;
   A blooming prose of rhyme and rot.

   It has not tasted the tension
   of gun-mental or smoke-aged bombs.
   There is much you could sacrifice
   for old-money tongues or notes of plum.

— • —

Isn't that the thick of it?

An outlet?
    Somebody to scream into the mouth of?
    To share scattered soundwaves and sink into the sea
    An abyss of desperate breaths and casual disposition to self-hating
harrows.

    Is it wrong to share the claws of clenched airways?
    Dust-tongued licks of terrified rage.

[The Sternum's Death Rattle]

Enter Stage Left: a bed of bones
    Rattling cracks of jacks on concrete,
    My grandmother's fact of Act Four Cancer.

Offstage: The Ribs
    Disjointed as they writhe,
    Blood eagled with railroad spikes and iron plates,
    Regal faced while the iron strikes hot.

[Do You Hear the Music?]

    It shakes silt onto hungry thieves—
    Ground guilt pressed into acrylic sheets.

The Needle Skips the Vein
Stage Left:
    An apology,
    dressed in starched paper pants.

[Audience Quiets.]

[SHE STILL SINGS.]

LITTLE PLEASURES

Carve every sin from my skin
    And when all that's left
    Is exhaustion and contempt,
    Do not mind the calcium-struck heart,
    or the gnawing
    unsatisfying end.
    I am nothing without the pieces carved away.
    Just bone, and rust, and an empty cage.

ENCASED

We speak of worship like sailors to the sea,
  With respect and anger and passion,
  Putting our fears into fragile figures,
  A method of coping with the daily strain,
  But the gods create the waves themselves,
  not our ability to coast them.

  Offering away the coarse caress of life,
  Encased and entombed.

THIS BODY IS NOT YOUR OWN.

Skin peels from my bone
  The muscle torn with viscera
  Breath grasping in my lungs, claws breaking my trachea.
  Anxiety was never less bitter—
  Shoulders popping, breaking in
  Clavical snapped times three again
  Nausea runs through like a blade—
  Should such a fight be done in vain?

— · —

RUM BOTTLE KISSES

It is simple to cast aside
    The desire that lies
    in the hollows of my chest.

    But once liquor presses upon my lips,
    My resolve is broken
    The stone wall tips.
    Am I burdened with rum-bottle kisses;
    Or do I crave something true and vicious?

— ◦ —

SILENT THREATS

But like a hunter in the leaves,
   It was me he'd find and bind,
   Dragging back with gentle hands
   Gentle eyes,
   The river, his tears, for me to swim—
   Hunt on the wall like a prized deer—
   You cannot leave.
   A loving mask to hide the fear.

   And like a fire,
   you'd burn away all of my senses,
   Leave an empty carcass that you could crawl in,
   A pelt and fire to keep you warm,
   A shield to mold to your form,
   in an unescaping grasp.

SEVENTEEN

Liquor licks my brain clean
  Of every single catastrophe
  Of worlds gone past,
  Of people who never last.

  But you survive the fight,
  And the desire for your touch
  Amplifies on drunken nights.
  The voice in my head,
  The Pounding of my heart.

  I'll drink to forget everything,
  The emotions that ignite
  When little can go right,
  But I'll never forget
  The darkness offset
  By the fear I get
  As you name hands in my head

— • —

CYCLIC

Blood-licked teeth, like a philistine fighter,
  Born again from destruction,
  Again from scraping grain
  Tradition has broken my bones
  and sent for me again.

— • —

(You Forgave Your Abuser, But Didn't Spare Me the Flashbacks)

I am ever so pleased,
   near cordially,
   to be of darling use to you.
   And happier so, that once my use ran out,
   Once my comfort was expended and left to dangle,
   Suspended over drawbridge kitchen sinks
   and left to rot.
   But should I wipe away your debris,
   And slip into the comfort of careful adoration?

   I will not sell your sugar-coated words, nor inject myself with this particular poison.
   You dug your own grave.

SIMPLE (DEROGATORY)

Call me devastating. Say my eyes rival tsunamis,
  Say the freckles across my skin are solar flares
  Tell me my lips will carve poetry from your heart,
  That my tongue will burn the psalms of the new world into existence.
  Pretty is such a *simple* word.
  Tell me I am the grace of the world.
  Declare my devastation in idolization.

— • —

To Forge a Sword from Blood.

I have no tolerance for being *saved*,
    Rather, a high disdain,
    From stone barriers barraged,
    Find sand left coating the shore.

    It leaves the same taste as the tongue when the body runs without
sleep,
    The same sedentary sediment that rings with iron-rich rage
    And righteous disgust.

Tragedies (2)

Sweet, vile nostalgia is bitter.
  A reminder of things once had,
  And yet the moon shines brighter, still
  Creating the tide's drawback.

  Silence befalls,
  A battlefield, a storm,
  The starlight covered with smoke and soot,
  And the only light is bolt flashes,
  as the ground collapses,
  and sink you will,
  Surrounded by the blood of your forefathers, still.

  Yet the storm blows through, and the moon shines bright,
  And the rising tides will lift you back to light,
  Through shadow and pain
  as her tides call your name
  The rain washes blood from broken hands,
  And the salted sea will sting.

  And it is a reminder, if nothing else, that you are alive,
  Like the splinters in your hands

or the heart beating—perhaps too fast—in your chest.
The clouds are still sweet,
watering anew,
and fires burn bright to make way for new life.
The stars—an ever-present map of the roads you'll soon travel;

There's a unifying silence—
What is a silver lining if not a thread
we weave ourselves to make amends?

So bask in the silence, the storm, and the fire,
Let the earth swallow you whole,
And let the air bring you higher.

I cannot explain the full feeling of it,
But these things make us human,
and we will pump blood into hard hearts again.

OCEAN SERENITY

Waves are a deadly beast,
    The ocean cold, yet filled with heart,
    A magical place where the worlds part,
    The water is alive, it's in our blood;

    Hiding in the showers next to the pool,
    Breaking into golf course greens,
    Talking about the boys who proved themselves tools,
    A hillside path,
    Snails galore,
    Sitting on rocks when we were bored;

    There's no remedy
    Nor Replacement,
    For a part of my heart is always yours,
    Nobody needs to know
    of nights alone,
    The Sisterhood we did once sow,
    Claiming bonds no one else could bear,
    Taking pieces of my soul,
    but leaving some of yours there;
    And I will say,

Without any need to call out your name,
Is that Ocean Serenity will
always be ours.

IT IS A GOOD DAY

to meditate in heartbreak.
    To stare at the ceiling as it crumbles,
    Each note brushing the ache under my breast.
    The torment of solitude crawling up from its rest
    And the sadness sinks
    Like a familiar friend
    As we teeter on the brink
    of accepting our dejection
    And greeting it with detest.

BETTER FORMS OF WORSHIP

I would carve your existence from my skin like
   ichor carves a demon's lips.
   Your blood dripping from my chin,
   Name gasped—my last breath,
   And maybe pride
   wouldn't be my sacrilege.
   Every inch stripped in your name like I'm
   blessing an altar with love and pain
   A roll-around of decadence is written in the stains:
   Of impudence and anger from the darker days
   But kept wrapped tight, and nurtured the same,
   We will always heal like a Phoenix from a flame.

   Take my soul and take my life—
   For her, it is not in vain,
   no matter my own bane.

BITTER ON THE TONGUE

I stare down the barrel of blurry eyes
    Iron: hollow / rash.
    Each slim picking the succulent taste of cinnamon
    sitting in throats to rot.

— • —

I AM PLAGUED BY DISCONTENT,

The unsettling press of my bones
  Heart collapsing in—
  Breaks.
  Reaches to combine itself once more,
  To fix what was once torn.

SANCTUARY STATE OF MIND

I wish I could be softer;
    I wish this kindness was not for show,
    I wish my boiling blood would burst from my arteries
    and spill
    Leaving venom as my martyr
    To break crystal skin and shed steeled lacerations,
    As silk soaks with generous subtlety,
    and Vying care.

    But my good heart is taut with tungsten ribs,
    And the battle to bless the lips with toxicants compacts.
    To fight to be good—
    Is that really even fair?
    When my iron-forged fists were built from despair,
    That I have to anguish in hiding my anger for the comfort of those
who failed,
    But I have always had to handle my pain.

    And some bathed in silk and sorrow have not the walls to fight,
    So my skin will break to make them safe.
    And in the corner of my mind,
    That kindness will survive,

While the vitriol will hold vigil for those who press pain.

A Promising Enterprise

May the chill of mortality rapture your flesh,
    Bygones boiling through your veins,
    They ricochet insecurities and school-born blooded hatred for it all.

    What hope am I to have in this?
    Ignorance is all but bliss—to lie in the abyss
    To dismiss the reasonable cause for concern—
    To stare into a cycle of constant aggression with no outlet for humanity,
    All at the whims of company policy.

    Nescience poisons the well and molds the masses to feeble lines,
    Hope is too often a disguise
    For traditional minds to hide behind
    And sully with falsities entwined with enterprise lies.

— • —

THE COST OF KEEPING PEACE

I have tiptoed for eternity,
  Around the bounds and needs of another,
  Taking care to give it,
  Protecting mirrored mansions, and sweeping the blows
  While my soles become broken glass from walking in the shards.

RESILIENCE

I am beyond *resilience*.
   What do I have to show for this,
   But a broken body?

   To be praised with penniless pleasantries,
   laughed upon and patronized,
   As if you are a part of the repartee
   not just the foundation of its stones.
   As if the damage done is a blessing all the same,
   the sweet kisses of broken backs.

   Can you feel how your cartilage creaks?

— • —

It Is Waiting For You

Can you hear it in the hallway?
Or the touch along your sacrum.
Leg

by

leg

as it steps into your hands?

It is a patient thing
Like bone spurs and battery,
Welling until there is nothing left to save.

— ◦ —

THERE IS SOMETHING IN YOUR BONES

A cold pulse beats through your skin as the candles take on a blackened glow.

The tremors of the earth, deep and all-knowing, still choked in binds as each tunnel and broken breath permeates your skin.
`There is something in your bones.`

Enshringed in flesh—unmoving
but wanting.
You are all that slithers and swarms, burrowing and breaking.
There is a hive in the waste,
A mountainous bound of skittering things—
It shutters under the weight of its many-legged darlings, fracturing
in ways that dust should not
As the nitrogen burrows into the soil with full collapse
tumbling in toxic waves of spoiled indulgence.
THE SMOKE BURNS INTO YOUR EYES, BUT THE COLD HAS NOT LEFT.

Instead, the form of a faceless king,
consuming all that lies beyond him.

You watch as his insides rip,
pores filling with blood and puss as he indulges evermore,
splitting like the fibers of fine bread,

and the ants crawl out

Ever hungry as he,

and they

consume.   .

THAT WHICH BURROWS INTO YOUR BONE PLAYS KIN TO SUCH THINGS.

A trickling sickness weaves into your tongue,

down your throat, and into your lungs,

Inching with insistent precision

A cage has bloomed in your gut and suffocated your screams.

And that which is cold builds you again as it sits within your bones

and feeds on hard-won calcium cracks and solid spurs.

THERE IS SOMETHING IN YOUR BONES,
and it is not She who spreads and schemes.

ACKNOWLEDGMENTS

Sinew and Sea was a long time coming.

I distinctly remember my mother having me read her poetry before school. It was an Emily Dickinson collection that still sits on my shelf to this day, prized and protected. Even with all of our ups and downs, she never stopped believing in me, which is more than I can say for myself. Her love of reading and writing was passed to me from birth. Her influence has made me who I am today, and I have to appreciate her for all that it is worth. Thank you for trying to save as much of my art as possible and for teaching me its worth.

This journey began a few years ago, with a naive approach to publishing and nearly falling for a vanity press. From day one, Rogelio—one of my best friends—was there to push and pressure me into finishing. Despite his (self-stated) lack of understanding regarding poetry, he has always been there to lovingly bully me into finishing *Sinew and Sea.*

(And just between us, despite what he says, he can understand poetry just fine.)

My darling partner Taliesin has watched my sleepless nights and handled the bombardment of poetry in our private discord server. Without their reminders to eat and rest, I would probably be a zombie by now.

Kamryn Boykin, my incredible sister, handpainted the cover art for *Sinew and Sea* in early 2023 and I could not be more pleased with it. Her time and effort absolutely blew me away and she will eternally be my favorite artist. We have grown so much from the two barely functioning young adults in Norman, Oklahoma. Every moment I have known her has been a blessing and I couldn't be more lucky to have her in my life.

Trinity Phan-Low is another woman that I am exponentially grateful for. She did the graphic design for *Sinew and Sea*'s cover in the midst of preparing for her college graduation, balancing her capstone project with everything life has thrown at her this year. She is so much stronger than she knows and deserves the recognition.

Finally, a thank you to somebody (or something) who has been with me step by step, forcing me to be productive. Lofi Girl, keep on studying dude. Your surprisingly involved lore keeps me going.

COVER ART AND GRAPHIC DESIGN

Kamryn Boykin is an American artist based in Idaho, where she is completing a Bachelors of Fine Art degree with an emphasis in Time-Based Media. She also has an Associates in Arts from Tulsa Community College in Oklahoma.
She can be found on Instagram @kamryn._.rose

Trinity Phan-Low is a Graphics, Game, and Character designer from California. She is obtaining her Bachelors of Science in Communication Design with a concentration in Game Design from Cal State University, Monterey Bay.
She can be found at her website www.tplportfolio.com or contacted at tphanlow@gmail.com

— · —

—— ❖ ——

—·—

Milton Keynes UK
Ingram Content Group UK Ltd.
UKHW012126221223
434840UK00004B/338

9 798218 277024